The Best Nest

Written by
Cath Jones

Illustrated by
Camila Carrossine

Madge sat on a huge bean bag and looked out at the birds. They were pecking at some seeds and nuts she had put on the window ledge.

"What can you see?" asked her sister, Fran.

"Nests," said Madge. "The garden is full of them. Look. There is one in the oak tree, another in the hedge and a little one in the holly bush."

"Oh," said Fran. "Nests! Is that all?"

She put on the TV. But it was so loud that all the birds flew away.

Madge was not happy.

"I wish I did not have to sleep in the same bedroom as you!" she said. "I wish I could sleep in a nest, like the birds. Then I would not have to put up with you."

Madge went out into the garden and had a little chat with a blackbird.

Then she began to gather up twigs and leaves.

"What are you up to now?" asked Fran.

"I'm going to have a nest just for me. No more sleeping in a bedroom with you!" Madge said.

Fran thought that was silly!

But Gran thought it would be fantastic to make a huge nest for Madge to sit in!

Gran got Mum and Dad to join in too!

Soon the nest was big and strong.

It was very soft too!

Then Gramps made a bridge from the girls' bedroom to the nest.

Madge sat in her nest. She had a picnic.

"This is the best nest," she called to all the birds. "And it is all just for me. There is no Fran in my nest!"

A robin came and had a look at the nest.
It sat on the edge.

Then a finch sat next to Madge.

Soon, the nest was full of birds. There was not much room for Madge at all!

A woodpecker gave Madge a little nudge.

"Budge up!" said Madge.

But the birds did not budge up.

Soon, Madge was right on the edge of her nest.

Then, three fat blue tits came to see what all the fuss was about.

"Oh no," said Madge. Then she fell out!

Madge went back to her bedroom. Fran was on the bed.

"Your best nest was too good!" said Fran. "The birds liked it too much! Why don't we make this into the best bedroom? Just for us."